LET'S COOK WITH
Noodles!

Delicious & Fun Noodle Dishes Kids Can Make

Nancy Tuminelly

Consulting Editor, Diane Craig, M.A./Reading Specialist

A Division of ABDO
ABDO
Publishing Company

visit us at www.abdopublishing.com

Published by ABDO Publishing Company, a division of ABDO, P.O. Box 398166, Minneapolis, Minnesota 55439.

Printed in the United States of America, North Mankato, Minnesota
062012
092012

 PRINTED ON RECYCLED PAPER

Editor: Liz Salzmann
Content Developer: Nancy Tuminelly
Cover and Interior Design and Production: Colleen Dolphin, Mighty Media, Inc.
Food Production: Desirée Bussiere
Photo Credits: Colleen Dolphin, Shutterstock, iStockphoto (Gary Milner, Dawna Stafford)

The following manufacturers/names appearing in this book are trademarks: Good Seasons® Italian All Natural Salad Dressing & Recipe Mix, KA-ME® Sesame Oil, Market Pantry® Chicken Broth, Market Pantry® Diced Tomatoes, Market Pantry® Pure Vanilla Extract, Market PAM® Baking Spray, Pyrex® Measuring Glass, Roundy's® Soy Sauce

Library of Congress Cataloging-in-Publication Data
Tuminelly, Nancy, 1952-
  Let's cook with noodles! : delicious & fun noodle dishes kids can make / Nancy Tuminelly.
    p. cm. -- (Super simple recipes)
  ISBN 978-1-61783-422-6
  1. Cooking (Pasta)--Juvenile literature. 2. Noodles--Juvenile literature. I. Title.
  TX809.M17T86 2013
  641.82'2--dc23
                            2011052195

Super SandCastle™ books are created by a team of professional educators, reading specialists, and content developers around five essential components—phonemic awareness, phonics, vocabulary, text comprehension, and fluency—to assist young readers as they develop reading skills and strategies and increase their general knowledge. All books are written, reviewed, and leveled for guided reading, early reading intervention, and Accelerated Reader® programs for use in shared, guided, and independent reading and writing activities to support a balanced approach to literacy instruction.

Note to Adult Helpers

Helping kids learn how to cook is fun! It's a great way to practice math and science. Cooking teaches kids about responsibility and boosts their confidence. Plus, they learn how to help out in the kitchen! The recipes in this book require adult assistance. Make sure there is always an adult around when kids are in the kitchen. Expect kids to make a mess, but also expect them to clean up after themselves. Most importantly, make the experience pleasurable by sharing and enjoying the food kids make.

Symbols

Knife
Always ask an adult to help you use knives.

Microwave
Be careful with hot food! Learn more on page 7.

Oven
Have an adult help put things into and take them out of the oven. Learn more on page 7.

Stovetop
Be careful around hot burners! Learn more on page 7.

Nuts
Some people can get very sick if they eat nuts.

Contents

Let's Cook
with Noodles!

Noodles are a favorite food around the world. The average person eats about 15½ pounds of noodles a year. They are healthy and **delicious**. And, they are easy to make!

Most noodles are made from wheat flour and water. Asian noodles are made with soy, rice, or buckwheat flour. Some noodles have egg in them. Italian noodles are called pasta. There are more than 600 kinds. Spaghetti is the most popular.

The recipes in this book are simple. It's fun using one main ingredient! Cooking teaches you about food, measuring, and following directions. Enjoy your tasty treats with your family and friends!

Think Safety!

- Ask an adult to help you use knives. Use a cutting board.

- Clean up spills to prevent accidents.

- Keep tools and **utensils** away from the edge of the table or counter.

- Use a step stool if you cannot reach something.

- Tie back long hair or wear a hat.

- Don't wear loose clothes. Roll up long **sleeves**.

- Keep a fire extinguisher in the cooking area.

Cooking Basics

Before you start...

- Get **permission** from an adult.

- Wash your hands.

- Read the recipe at least once.

- Set out all the ingredients and tools you will need.

When you're done...

- Cover food with plastic wrap or aluminum foil. Use **containers** with lids if you have them.

- Wash all of the dishes and **utensils**.

- Put all of the ingredients and tools back where you found them.

- Clean up your work space.

Using the Microwave

- Use microwave-safe dishes.

- Never put aluminum foil or metal in the microwave.

- Start with a short cook time. If it's not enough, cook it some more.

- Use oven mitts when taking things out of the microwave.

- Stop the microwave to stir liquids during heating.

Using the Stovetop

- Turn pot handles away from the burners and the edge of the stove.

- Use the temperature setting in the recipe.

- Use pot holders to handle hot pots and pans.

- Do not leave metal **utensils** in pots.

- Don't put anything except pots and pans on or near the burners.

- Use a timer. Check the food and cook it more if needed.

Using the Oven

- Use the temperature setting in the recipe.

- Preheat the oven while making the recipe.

- Use oven-safe dishes.

- Use pot holders or oven mitts to handle baking sheets and dishes.

- Do not touch oven doors. They can be very hot.

- Set a timer. Check the food and bake it more if needed.

A microwave, stovetop, and oven are very useful for cooking food. But they can be **dangerous** if you are not careful. Always ask an adult for help.

Measuring

Wet Ingredients

Set a measuring cup on the counter. Add the liquid until it reaches the amount you need. Check the measurement from eye level.

Dry Ingredients

Use a spoon to put the dry ingredient in the measuring cup or spoon. Put more than you need in the measuring cup or spoon. Run the back of a dinner knife across the top. This removes the extra.

Moist Ingredients

Moist ingredients are things such as brown sugar and dried fruit. They need to be packed down into the measuring cup. Keep packing until the ingredient reaches the measurement line.

Do You Know This = That?

There are different ways to measure the same amount.

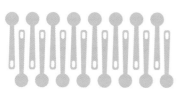 =

3 teaspoons   1 tablespoon

 =

4 tablespoons   ¼ cup

 =

5 tablespoons   1 teaspoon   ⅓ cup

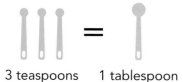 =

16 tablespoons   1 cup

=

1 cup   8 ounces

=

1 stick of butter   ½ cup

 =

2 cups   1 pint

 =

4 cups   1 quart   2 quarts   ½ gallon

Cooking Terms

Mix
Combine ingredients with a mixing spoon. *Stir* is another word for mix.

Dice or Cube
Cut something into small squares with a knife.

Chop
Cut something into very small pieces with a knife.

Boil
Heat liquid until it begins to bubble.

Drain
Remove liquid using a strainer or colander.

Peel
Remove skin from a fruit or vegetable. Use a peeler if needed.

Slice
Cut something into thin pieces with a knife.

Grate
Shred something into small pieces using a grater.

Noodles for One

1. Put 1 cup of water in a small, microwave-safe dish. It should have a flat bottom. Microwave on high for 2½ minutes or until the water boils.

2. Add ¼ teaspoon salt and ¼ teaspoon vegetable oil.

3. Put 2 ounces of small noodles into the bottom of the dish. Spread them out so they make one layer.

4. Microwave on medium for 10 to 12 minutes or until the water is gone. The noodles will be soft.

5. Top the noodles with butter or your favorite pasta sauce!

Tools

liquid measuring cup

sharp knife

peeler & corer

cutting board

oven mitts

colander

spoon

timer

mixing spoon

dry measuring cups

measuring spoons

9 x 13-inch baking dish

fork

frying pan

pot holders

aluminum foil

plastic wrap

strainer

mixing bowls

whisk

large pot

Ingredients

peas

mandarin oranges

raisins

chili with beans

eggs

whole kernel corn

apples

pineapple chunks

lemon

mushrooms

creamy salad dressing

green bell pepper

onion

firm tofu

fresh parsley

garlic cloves

celery

sour cream

carrots

milk

black olives

butter

green onions

Genoa salami

mayonnaise

spinach

tomato sauce

fussili pasta

macaroni noodles

mozzarella cheese

egg noodles

Italian dressing mix

sesame oil

sugar

bow-tie pasta

large pasta shells

soba noodles

soy sauce

cooked chicken

olive oil

vanilla extract

ricotta cheese

parmesan cheese

diced tomatoes

salt & pepper

chicken broth

peanut butter

non-stick cooking spray

crushed red pepper

cinnamon

nutmeg

ginger

Fruity Noodle Salad

A tasty surprise to serve any time!

Makes 8 to 10 servings

ingredients

16 ounces fusilli pasta

15-ounce can mandarin oranges, drained

20-ounce can pineapple chunks, drained

¼ cup green onion, chopped

½ cup creamy salad dressing

tools

large pot

pot holders

strainer or colander

measuring cups

sharp knife

cutting board

mixing spoon

large mixing bowl

plastic wrap

1. Cook the noodles according to the instructions on the package. Drain the noodles. Rinse them with cold water.

2. Put the noodles, oranges, pineapple, green onion, and salad dressing in the large mixing bowl. Mix well.

3. Cover the bowl with plastic wrap. Put it in the refrigerator for at least an hour.

A delicious meal without the wait!

Makes 4 servings

ingredients

8 ounces fusilli pasta

1 tablespoon olive oil

1 onion, chopped

3 garlic cloves, sliced

8 cups baby spinach

3½ cups mushrooms, sliced

14-ounce can diced tomatoes

½ teaspoon crushed red pepper

½ teaspoon salt

¼ teaspoon pepper

¾ cup ricotta cheese

tools

large pot	measuring cups & spoons
pot holders	
strainer or colander	frying pan
	cutting board
large mixing bowl	mixing spoon
sharp knife	timer

1 Cook the noodles according to the instructions on the package. Drain the noodles. Put them in the large mixing bowl.

2 Heat the oil in the frying pan for 1 minute over medium heat. Add the onion and garlic. Cook for 4 to 6 minutes. Stir often.

3 Add the spinach, mushrooms, tomatoes, red pepper, salt, and pepper. Turn the heat to medium high. Cook for 4 minutes while stirring. Remove from heat.

4 Add the spinach mixture to the noodles. Stir well. Spoon evenly onto four plates. Add 3 tablespoons ricotta cheese to each serving.

Triple Cheese Shells

Yummy cheese and noodles make the best Italian meal!

Makes 12 shells

ingredients

12 ounces large pasta shells

2 cups ricotta cheese

⅓ cup parmesan cheese, grated

1 cup mozzarella cheese, grated

⅓ cup fresh parsley, chopped

nutmeg

4 to 5 cups tomato sauce

tools

grater

large pot

pot holders

strainer or colander

measuring cups

sharp knife

cutting board

mixing spoon

large mixing bowl

spoon

9 × 13-inch baking dish

aluminum foil

oven mitts

timer

1 Preheat the oven to 350 **degrees**.

2 Cook the noodles according to the instructions on the package. Drain the noodles. Set them aside.

3 Put the three cheeses, parsley, and a **dash** of nutmeg in a large bowl. Mix well.

4 Carefully fill the shells with the cheese mixture.

5 Cover the bottom of the baking dish with 2 cups of the tomato sauce. Put the filled shells over the sauce. Pour the rest of the sauce on top. Cover the dish with aluminum foil.

6 Bake for 30 minutes. Remove the dish from the oven. Let it sit for 5 minutes before serving.

Corny Chili Macaroni

A hearty south-of-the-border pasta treat!

Makes 4 servings

ingredients

4 ounces macaroni noodles
1 tablespoon butter
1 green bell pepper, chopped
½ medium onion, chopped
15-ounce can chili with beans
8.75-ounce can
    whole kernel corn, drained
1 teaspoon salt
1 teaspoon pepper

tools

large pot	cutting board
pot holders	mixing spoon
strainer or colander	measuring spoons
large frying pan with cover	timer
sharp knife	

1   Cook the noodles according to the instructions on the package. Drain the noodles. Set them aside.

2   Melt the butter in the frying pan on medium heat. Add the green pepper and onion. Cook until the vegetables are soft. Stir often.

3   Stir in the chili, corn, salt, and pepper. Turn the heat to low. Cook for 5 minutes.

4   Stir in the noodles. Cover the pan and cook for 5 minutes.

5   Remove the pan from the heat. Put the macaroni in four bowls. Serve it warm.

Apple Noodle Kugel

A sweet noodle delight for a snack or dessert!

Makes 8 servings

ingredients

16 ounces egg noodles

½ cup butter, melted

8 eggs, beaten

½ cup raisins

1 teaspoon vanilla extract

4 teaspoons cinnamon

⅓ cup sugar

2 teaspoons salt

non-stick cooking spray

3 to 4 apples, cored and sliced

tools

peeler & corer

large pot

pot holders

strainer or colander

mixing bowls

mixing spoon

fork or whisk

measuring cups & spoons

9 × 13-inch baking dish

sharp knife

cutting board

oven mitts

timer

1   Preheat the oven to 350 **degrees**. Cook the noodles according to the instructions on the package. Drain the noodles.

2   Put the noodles in a large mixing bowl. Mix in the melted butter.

3   Stir the beaten eggs into the noodles. Add the raisins, vanilla, cinnamon, sugar, and salt. Mix well.

4   Cover the baking dish lightly with cooking spray. Pour in the noodle mixture. Spread it out evenly.

5   Arrange the apple slices on top. Bake 45 to 60 minutes. The top should be golden brown. Let it cool for 5 minutes before serving.

3

4

5

Peanutty Asian Noodles

A scrumptious change from Italian pasta!

Makes 4 servings

ingredients

8.8-ounce package soba
 noodles

2 tablespoon sesame oil

8 ounces firm tofu, cut into
 1-inch (3 cm) cubes

1 tablespoon ginger

2 tablespoons peanut butter

1 tablespoon sugar

2 tablespoons soy sauce

juice from ½ lemon

tools

large pot

strainer or
colander

pot holders

measuring
spoons

frying pan

sharp knife

cutting board

large mixing
bowl

mixing spoon

timer

1   Cook the noodles according to the instructions on the package. Drain the noodles. Rinse them with cold water.

2   Put 1 tablespoon sesame oil in the frying pan. Cook on medium heat. Add the tofu. Fry until the tofu is brown and **crispy**. Stir occasionally. Add the ginger. Fry for 3 minutes.

3   Put the peanut butter, sugar, soy sauce, lemon juice, and 1 tablespoon sesame oil in a large bowl. Mix well.

4   Add the noodles and tofu into the peanut butter mixture. Stir until the noodles and tofu are covered.

TIP: Also try it with cubed chicken instead of tofu!

Nona's Noodle Soup

Everyone loves Grandma's recipe!

Makes 4 to 6 servings

ingredients

1 tablespoon butter

1 tablespoon olive oil

1 cup carrots, peeled & sliced

1 cup celery, chopped

1 medium onion, diced

1 cup mushrooms, sliced

salt and pepper

8 cups chicken broth

3 cups egg noodles

3 cups cooked chicken, cubed

3 tablespoons fresh parsley, chopped

tools

large pot

measuring cups & spoons

sharp knife

cutting board

peeler & corer

mixing spoon

pot holders

spoon

timer

1 Melt the butter and olive oil in a large pot. Use medium-low heat.

2 Add the carrots, celery, onion, mushrooms, and a **pinch** of salt and pepper. Cook for 10 minutes. Stir often.

3 Add the broth. Turn the heat to high. When the broth boils, slowly stir in the noodles. Cook for 9 minutes or until noodles are soft.

4 Turn the heat to medium-low. Add the chicken and parsley. Cook for 5 minutes.

5 Carefully taste the soup with a clean spoon. Add more **seasoning** if necessary.

Italian Pasta Supreme

A delicious salad that is a meal in itself!

Makes 12 servings

ingredients

16 ounces bow-tie pasta
2 tablespoons milk
1 cup sour cream
1 cup mayonnaise
1 packet Italian dressing mix
1 cup peas
4 ounces black olives, sliced
1 cup Genoa salami, cubed
¾ cup green onion, chopped
¾ cup celery, chopped
½ cup fresh parsley, chopped

tools

large pot
strainer or colander
pot holders
mixing bowls
measuring cups

measuring spoons
mixing spoon
sharp knife
cutting board
plastic wrap
timer

1   Cook the noodles according to the instructions on the package. Drain the noodles. Rinse them with cold water.

2   Make the dressing. Put the milk, sour cream, mayonnaise, and Italian dressing mix in a medium bowl. Mix well.

3   Mix the noodles, peas, olives, salami, green onion, celery, and parsley in a large bowl. Pour all but ½ cup of the dressing over the noodle mixture. Put the extra ½ cup of dressing in the refrigerator.

4   Stir the salad well. Cover the bowl with plastic wrap. Leave it in the refrigerator overnight.

5   Stir before serving. Add extra dressing if necessary.

Glossary

container – something that other things can be put into.

crispy – hard, thin, and easy to break.

dangerous – able or likely to cause harm or injury.

dash – a very small amount added with a quick, downward shake.

degree – the unit used to measure temperature.

delicious – very pleasing to taste or smell.

permission – when a person in charge says it's okay to do something.

pinch – the amount you can hold between your thumb and one finger.

seasoning – something, such as herbs, spices, or salt, added to food to make it taste better.

sleeve – the part of a piece of clothing that covers some or all of the arm.

utensil – a tool used to prepare or eat food.